PLAYING IN STILLNESS
A Collection of Guided Mindfulness Practices

Molly Schreiber, Melissa Hyde, and Paula Purcell

Illustrations & Graphics by Kari Bahl, Paula Purcell, and Lora Fuller

www.challengetochangeinc.com

CREDITS

ORIGINAL MEDITATIONS
Molly Schreiber, Melissa Hyde, and Paula Purcell

ORIGINAL ILLUSTRATIONS & GRAPHICS
Kari Bahl, Paula Purcell, and Lora Fuller

Introduction

While the exact birthdate of meditation is not known, scholars and archaeologists agree that it has been practiced by humans for thousands of years. The earliest written documents of meditation were recorded in India in 1500 BCE, and the practice expanded from India into China sometime between 600 and 400 BCE.

Meditation is a common practice today, and its benefits are frequently lauded by those in the medical, biological sciences, and mental healthcare fields. These benefits include:

- **reduced stress and anxiety**
- **stronger emotional health and stability**
- **increased awareness of the physical body**
- **improved attention span and memory retention**
- **greater feelings of empathy and kindness towards ourselves and others**
- **healthier sleep patterns**

All people; no matter their age, ethnicity, socio-economic status, or religious background; can reap these benefits when they practice meditation.

Childhood experts, however, often emphasize the strong impact meditation can have on children in helping to reduce anxiety, promote positive self-esteem, and improve social-emotional regulation skills.

One of the most powerful aspects of yoga is that it can be practiced anytime, anywhere, by absolutely anyone. And it doesn't cost a thing!

A common misconception about meditation is that those who meditate do so with a completely blank mind. This is absolutely not true.

The practice of meditation is simply learning to sit with the thoughts that enter your mind without feeling the need to immediately react to any emotions or impulses that arise. It is learning to let thoughts enter and leave your consciousness while using deep breaths to refocus your mind and calm your physical body.

While it is possible to practice meditation in absolute silence, many find it helpful to listen to peaceful music or calm words while meditating in order to help quiet and still the mind.

This book is a compilation of guided meditation and visualization stories we use at Challenge to Change to help provide a focal point for the mind when engaging in meditation. You will find that sometimes these are referred to as meditations, and others times we use the expression guided mindfulness practice. These are used interchangeably and mean the same thing.

We hope you find the stories in this book both helpful and pleasurable. We certainly have!

Thank you for allowing us to be a part of your mindfulness journey.

Namaste,

The Challenge to Change Team

How to use This book

We have included a wide variety of scripts in this book to help you lead a guided mindfulness or meditation practice for yourself and others. The theme for each guided mindfulness practice can be found in the table of contents, as well as at the top of each script. Our meditation practices are intended to be accessible to people of all ages.

You will find that some of these scripts are short, while others are quite lengthy. This is to give you a variety of options to choose from in order to best suit the needs of your intended audience.

Here are a few tips for leading an effective meditation or guided mindfulness practice:

- Choose a calm, quiet place to lead your practice. Dim lighting is recommended.
- Select a script that connects with you so that it feels authentic when you are reading it aloud.
- Read in a natural tone of voice at a slow and steady pace.
- Calm and center yourself before leading the practice so that your audience can internalize the tranquility exuding from you.
- Quiet music playing in the background can add to the overall experience.
- Pay attention to any nonverbal cues coming from your listeners, and adjust to their needs. Ad lib the script as necessary.

Each of the scripts includes an introduction to help settle your audience and prepare them for the meditation ahead. They also each include a scripted ending to bring your listeners back to a seated position for you to close the practice.

These introductions and closings are suggestions only. While you are welcome to use the introductions and closings provided, we recommend you experiment with finding the words and expressions that you enjoy using to open and close your meditation practices.

Enjoy your journey into meditation and mindfulness.
May it be filled with peace, love, and joy.

Table of Contents

Floating on a Cloud

✝ A peaceful journey through the sky to your favorite place.

Begin to take deep inhales and exhales in and out through your nose. As you breathe, start to feel your body relax, your mind unwind, and your heartbeat slow.

As you listen to my words, remember to keep taking deep inhales in through your nose, feeling the air move deep into your belly, and exhale back out through your nose. Do this three more times:

Inhale . . . Exhale.

Inhale . . . Exhale.

Inhale . . . Exhale.

As you continue to breathe deeply and slowly, feel your smart mind connect to your kind heart and calm your body.

With your smart mind, begin to imagine that you are floating on a cloud — a big, fluffy white cloud. Notice how comfortable the cloud feels as it lifts you high into the sky. Know that you are completely safe on your cloud. This cloud has been made especially for you and your safe adventure.

As the cloud takes you higher into the sky, visualize in your mind where you want the cloud to take you. You can go anywhere you want — just ask your cloud to take you there.

As the cloud carries you to your special place, you can tell it to go higher or lower. You can tell it to go faster or slower. This cloud is your special cloud; it was made especially for you.

As your cloud takes you to your special place, notice how you feel. What does this journey do to your kind heart? Do you feel calm . . . excited . . . happy . . . peaceful?

This good feeling is always inside of you. You can feel it at any time, just by closing your eyes and connecting your smart mind to your kind heart and your calm body.

As your cloud comes to your special place, peek over the side of the cloud and look down on what is below.

What do you see?

What do you hear?

What do you feel?

Visualize all this clearly in your mind.

Now it is time for you to return from your special place. Ask your cloud to take you back. Remember that on your return home, you can ask your cloud to travel fast or slow; high or low. You are in control of your safe journey.

Ask your cloud to return you to where you are now. As your cloud slowly descends from the sky, take a deep breath in through your nose, and exhale it back out. Do this three more times:

Inhale . . . Exhale.

Inhale . . . Exhale.

Inhale . . . Exhale.

After your final exhale, stretch your arms up over your head and smile.

Rainbow Meditation

+ A colorful visualization focusing on the seven chakras and positive affirmations.

Make your body comfortable. Lie on the your back with your hands at your sides or resting gently on your belly. Stretch your legs out long and relax your feet. Take a deep breath in through your nose . . . and softly let it out. Close your eyes and feel your body start to slow down.

Take another deep breath in through your nose, then slowly exhale.

Continue to take deep breaths in and out as you relax your body and listen to my voice.

Imagine there is a big, beautiful rainbow in front of you. See its vibrant colors stretching across the sky: Red, orange, yellow, green, blue and purple.

Begin to see the red in the rainbow glowing brighter than any of the other colors. There is red light shining all around you, bathing you in its color. Breathe in deeply to inhale the color red and feel it fill your body from the top of your head to the tips of your toes. Think to yourself, "I am safe." You know this is true - you are supported and protected by the earth and all who care about you. Whisper to yourself, "I feel safe."

Now watch the color red begin to fade, and imagine the color orange is now beginning to glow. Soon the orange light is all around you. Breathe in the bright orange color and imagine it moving through your body to softly settle in the bottom of your belly. Think to yourself, "I am calm." Feel your body continue to relax, and focus your attention on all the good thoughts and feelings that are inside of you right now. Think to yourself, "I am at peace."

Let the orange light go back inside the rainbow, and imagine the color yellow beginning to glow brightly like the sun. The yellow is soon bathing the world around you with its golden light. Breathe in the yellow, and feel the light coat your throat and mouth like honey with its sunny glaze. Imagine the golden light moving down your throat into your stomach where it begins to sparkle and dance like twinkling fairy lights. Think to yourself, "I am powerful." Know this is true: You are strong and capable of doing anything you set your mind to. Think to yourself, "I am confident."

Now let the golden yellow light fade, and in your mind, watch the color green in the rainbow start to glow. The color slowly grows from the soft fuzzy green of new spring grass to the vibrant green of shiny leaves on a hot summer's day. Soon there is green light all around you. Breathe deeply to inhale the color green right into the center of your heart. Visualize that green light beating with love inside of your heart and think to yourself, "My family and friends love me, and I love them." Picture all the special people in your life and feel your heart continue to grow with love. Think to yourself, "I am loved."

Let the green light go back into the rainbow, and bring your attention to the color blue. It is a pale blue, and as you watch, the soft light begins to shimmer and sparkle. It glitters and flashes brighter and brighter until it gently leaps out of the rainbow to wrap its ethereal light all around you. It dances and swirls in the air. Take a deep breath in and feel its delicate texture wrap itself inside your throat. Smile and think to yourself, "People listen to me when I speak." You have amazing ideas to share with the world and truths to be told. Think to yourself, "I am heard."

As you exhale, the dancing blue light begins to recede and return to the rainbow, the purple on the rainbow begins to glow, and its glorious hue is soon all around you. It is a deep purple - the color of plump, ripe plums and velvety violets. Breathe in this rich purple color and feel it come to settle in the space between your eyes. Think to yourself, "I have a great imagination." You are a truly special person with wonderful, original ideas. Whisper to yourself, "I am knowing."

Finally, see the entire rainbow start to glow with all of its colors shining brightly in the sky. Picture yourself twirling and dancing in all the colors of the rainbow and think to yourself, "I am always learning, I am always growing." Hug in the colors of the rainbow and think to yourself, "I am capable."

Continue to breathe deeply, and in your mind, imagine the rainbow slowly starting to lift up higher and higher into the sky, then drift away. There are puffy clouds overhead, and a soft breeze blowing. You are at peace; you feel whole and complete.

Slowly begin to wiggle your fingers and toes, bringing awareness back to your physical body. Reach your arms up overhead, as far away from your toes as you can, and give your body a nice, big stretch. Make your body nice and long, then bend your knees and hug them tightly into your chest. Squeeze yourself into a ball, and then roll over onto your right side. Rest here for a moment before carefully bringing yourself up to a seated position with your hands at heart center for our close of practice.

Kids' Rainbow Meditation

✚ A shorter version of our rainbow meditation.

Make your body comfortable. Take a deep breath in . . . and out. Close your eyes and feel your body relax.

Take another deep breath in through your nose, then slowly let it back out through your nose.

Continue to take deep breaths in and out as you calm your body and listen to my voice.

Imagine there is a big, beautiful rainbow in front of you. See its vibrant colors stretching across the sky: Red, orange, yellow, green, blue and purple.

Begin to see the red in the rainbow glow brighter than any of the other colors. There is red light glowing all around you, bathing you in its color. Breathe deeply to inhale the color red and think to yourself, "I am safe." Whisper to yourself, "I feel safe."

Watch the color red begin to fade, and imagine the color orange is glowing brightly now. The orange light is all around you. Breathe in the color orange and think to yourself, "I am calm." Feel your body continue to relax and think to yourself, "I am peaceful."

Next, imagine the color yellow is glowing brightly like the sun. The color yellow is bathing the world in its golden light. Breathe in the yellow. Think to yourself, "I am powerful." Know this is true; that you are capable and strong. Think to yourself, "I am confident."

Now let the golden yellow light fade, and in your mind watch the color green in the rainbow begin to glow brighter. Soon, there is green all around you. Breathe deeply to inhale the color green. Think to yourself, "My family and friends love me, and I love them." Feel your heart fill with love, and think to yourself, "I am loved."

Let the green light go back into the rainbow, and bring your attention to the color blue. It is a light blue, and as you watch, the blue begins to shimmer and sparkle. The color blue wraps its light around you. Take a deep breath in and think to yourself, "People listen to me when I speak." Think to yourself, "I feel heard."

As the blue color fades, the purple on the rainbow begins to glow and its glorious hue is soon all around you. Breathe in the color purple and think to yourself, "I have a great imagination." You are a special person with wonderful, new ideas. Think to yourself, "I feel creative."

Finally, see the entire rainbow start to glow with all of its colors shining brightly. Picture yourself dancing in the colors of the rainbow and think to yourself, "I am always learning, I am always growing." Hug in the colors of the rainbow and think to yourself, "I am wise."

Continue to breathe deeply, and in your mind, imagine the rainbow slowly starting to lift higher and higher up into the sky, then drift away. There are puffy clouds overhead, and a soft breeze blowing. You are at peace, you feel whole and complete.

Slowly start to wiggle your fingers and toes, beginning to bring your body back to the present . . .

Mantra Mindfulness Practice

A meditation reminding us about the power of positive thinking and the many ways we can send our brains and hearts words of love and encouragement.

Lie on your back and relax your body. Straighten your legs and allow your feet to fall open naturally. Rest your arms at your sides or on your belly. Feel your shoulders and spine melt into the earth. Softly close your eyes.

Remember to come to your breath. Begin to take deep inhales and exhales in and out through your nose. Feel your body continue to relax, your mind unwind, and your heartbeat slow as you focus on taking deep breaths in and out through your nose.

Breathe in through your nose . . . and out. Breathe in . . . and out.

Mantras are words you say over and over to yourself in order to help your thinking become more positive. Mantras begin with the words, "I am", and the third word is what you want to become.

There are so many wonderful mantras that can help us think more positively about ourselves and the world around us. Today we are going to go through several of these mantras. After I say each mantra, please repeat it in your mind quietly or whisper it softly to yourself.

Are you ready? **"** *I am safe.*
I am grounded.
I am healthy.
I am strong. **"**

" *I am enough.*
I am courageous.
I am creative.
I am talented. **"**

" *I am calm.*
I am trying.
I am cooperative.
I am knowing. **"**

> *I am loving.*
> *I am grateful.*
> *I am friendly.*
> *I am joyful.*

> *I am respectful.*
> *I am kind.*
> *I am honest.*
> *I am positive.*

> *I am smart.*
> *I am responsible.*
> *I am unique.*
> *I am beautiful.*

> *I am peaceful.*
> *I am trustworthy.*
> *I am powerful.*
> *I am awesome.*

Our brains are powerful and amazing, and we can make them even more powerful and amazing by sending our brains positive messages. Our brains love mantras. The more often we tell our brains these positive messages, the happier and more confident we become. The happier and more confident we are, the kinder we become. When this happens, we become the best versions of ourselves.

Now pick a mantra that you really liked. Say it over and over in your brain. Keep saying it over and over until you hear the sound of the singing bowl telling you to come back to the present moment . . .

Boat Meditation

✚ A journey of self-empowerment and tranquility at sea.

Take a moment to find your most comfortable position. Lie down on the floor with your legs loose and long and your arms relaxed at your sides. Turn your palms up towards the sky and open your heart to receive this time of gentle peace.

Take a deep cleansing breath in through your nose . . . then slowly release and let it out. As you exhale, feel your entire body relax even further. Take another breath in . . . and let it out. Continue to breathe deeply at your own pace. Notice how your stomach expands with each inhale, and then slowly sinks towards the earth as you exhale.

As I count down from five to one, allow your body to grow heavy and calm.

5 . . . Notice the stillness in your hands and feet. Release any tension you have been holding on to.

4 . . . Allow your arms and legs to feel heavy and at rest.

3 . . . Relax your face, allowing any tension to fade away.

2 . . . Let your entire body grow heavy and sink towards the earth.

1 . . .

Now imagine you are walking alone on a white, sandy beach that stretches as far as your eyes can see. Feel the powdery, warm sand beneath your feet as you walk towards the crystal blue sea. Hear the sound of the gentle waves as they break onto the shore and slide back out.

The heat of the afternoon sun kisses your skin and fills your whole body with warmth and comfort. You feel the delicate ocean breeze brush softly across your skin. The air smells clean and crisp, and you can taste the subtle salt of the sea on your lips.

A small, wooden canoe is waiting for you on the shoreline. As you approach the boat, you grab the paddle that has been left inside and slowly climb aboard. The canoe immediately feels safe; almost as if it was built just for you. You push the paddle into the sand, gently guiding the boat out to sea and towards the brilliant red sunset ahead of you.

The calm waves hug the boat, pulling it away from the sandy beach, leading you further and further out to sea. Feeling completely safe and content, you set your paddle down and slide off of the seat to lie down in the bottom of the boat where you can rest.

You close your eyes. You feel embraced and protected by the curved sides of the boat. The waves gently cradle you as if the ocean was a mother rocking her newborn baby to sleep. Your body feels light, and you allow any stress onto which you have been holding to float away. You feel completely at peace.

After a short time, you wake and move back to your seat. You pick up the wooden paddle and dip it into the teal blue water, gently steering the boat back towards the shore. With a few deep strokes of the paddle and the push of a wave from behind, the vibration of the boat bottom against the sandy shoreline lets you know you've arrived. You come to a slow stop back on the beach.

Now, as I count from one to five, slowly begin to bring your awareness back to the present moment.

1 . . . Bring your attention to your breath. Take a deep inhale . . . and as you release, notice how relaxed and light you feel.

2 . . . Begin to bring movement back to your body by gently wiggling your fingers and toes.

3 . . . Stretch your arms overhead and take in another deep breath. As you exhale, wrap your arms around your knees and bring them into your chest.

4 . . . If it feels right, gently release and roll over onto your right side.

5 . . . In your own time, make your way back to an easy seated position for our close of practice.

Kindness Meditation

Close your eyes and begin taking deep breaths in through your nose and back out through your nose. As you inhale, feel the air move deep into your belly. As you exhale, feel the air leave your belly and move along the back of your throat and out your nose.

Continue to breathe. As you inhale and exhale, feel your body relax, your mind unwind, and your heartbeat slow. Remember that when we concentrate on breathing slowly and deeply, we slow our heartbeats, and then we slow our minds.

Breathe in through your nose . . . and out.

Think of something kind that you have done for someone recently. Maybe you helped a friend or a teacher at school. Maybe your act of kindness was something you did for a family member at home. How did it feel to do something kind for someone else?

Now think about something kind that someone else has recently done for you. Maybe someone said something nice to you. Maybe someone gave you a hug or invited you to play. Maybe the act of kindness was a family member helping you with your homework or cooking your favorite meal. How did it make you feel when something really nice was done for you?

Kindness always makes people feel good. Our hearts grow full when we receive kind words or actions, and they also grow when we do kind things for others. Being kind is always the right choice to make. All acts of kindness — big and small — make our world a better place.

As you continue to take deep breaths in and out through your nose, think of something kind that you can do for someone else today. Maybe it is some kind words that you could say to a friend, or maybe it is some kind way that you could be helpful at home or at school.

Picture yourself doing something kind for someone else, and make a promise to yourself to complete that act of kindness today.

Remember that we always want to make the world around us better than the way we found it. One of the best ways we can do that is by spreading kindness.

Now slowly start to wiggle your fingers and toes, and awaken yourself to your surroundings. Reach your hands up high over your head, as far away from your toes as you can. Then draw your knees into your chest and gently rock side to side.

Slowly rock to the side. Come to rest on the right side of your body, tucked into a small cocoon, just like a caterpillar would before it becomes a butterfly. While you're on your side, think of that one kind thing you are going to do today.

When you're ready, come up to your crisscross yogi-sauce. Put your hands at your heart center and smile.

Releasing Meditation

A lesson in how we have the power to let go of any
negative thoughts or feelings we have been holding on
to in order to create space for happier things.

Close your eyes. Begin to take deep inhales and exhales; in through your nose and back out. As you breathe, start to feel your mind relax, your body unwind, and your heartbeat slow. Breathe in . . . and breathe out.

Begin to visualize an image of yourself holding on to three balloons. Picture with great detail the colors of these three balloons. See the shapes of these three balloons vividly in your mind.

Visualize that each balloon represents something you are hanging on to that does not serve you. Something that you don't want in your life anymore.

Maybe you are holding on to a negative thought or feeling that you want to release. Perhaps you have been feeling frustrated by something that is hard to do, or you have been angry with someone about something they said or something they forgot. Notice in your mind what negative thoughts or feelings you have been holding on to.

It does not serve us to hold on to negative thoughts and feelings. Keeping negativity inside of us makes us feel badly about ourselves. Sometimes holding on to negative thoughts and feelings makes us act unkindly toward others.

But we can let these negative thoughts and feelings go. Visualize your three balloons and imagine that each one holds a negative thought or feeling that you want to get rid of.

Now notice the strings that connect the balloons to your hand. Notice how tightly your hand is holding on to the strings. Slowly and carefully begin to loosen your grip on the strings of the balloons. Notice how as you loosen your grip, the balloons slip out of your hand and begin to float up into the air.

Watch as each balloon goes higher . . . and higher . . . and higher away from you and up into the sky. Notice how small the balloons become as they get farther and farther away from you. Notice how much better you feel.

Look down at your hands, and notice how open they are. Notice how light they feel.

Now your hands are open to receiving something else; maybe something that makes you happier. Remember that when you let go of what does not serve you, you have room to do and think the things that make you happier.

Now think of three things that make you happier. Take time to visualize each one.

When you are finished thinking of three things that make you happy, breathe in and breathe out. Breathe in . . . breathe out . . . and smile.

Metta Mindfulness Practice

✚ A practice in spreading love and kindness to ourselves, people that we love, and those we don't like very much.

Take a deep inhale through your nose . . . and exhale back out through your nose. Take another deep inhale through your nose, feeling the air move deep into your belly, and exhale back out through your nose.

Today we're going to practice Metta Mindfulness. Metta is the practice of spreading love and kindness. Spreading love and kindness is very important to do because it helps make the world a happier and more peaceful place. It's very important for us to practice Metta on ourselves, to those that we love, and to those that we don't like very much.

You can do Metta anytime you want. You can do it while you're waiting in line, you can do it while you're riding in the car, or you can do it while you're sitting at your desk. All that you need in order to practice Metta is your smart mind and these four phrases:

May you be happy.
May you be healthy.
May you feel loved.
May you be safe.

It is always important to practice Metta on ourselves first, because it is only when we feel happy and loved that we can share happiness and love with others. So I want you to think about a picture of yourself.
Maybe it's your school picture, maybe it's a picture you took with your family, or maybe it's a picture of you doing something silly.

Visualize that picture. Now I want you to say the four phrases to yourself as I say them out loud:

May I be happy.
May I be healthy.
May I feel loved.
May I be safe.

(Repeat 1x)

It's so important to practice Metta on ourselves before we practice it on others. When we feel loved ourselves, then we can practice Metta on others whom we love very much too.

Now think about someone that you love very much. Maybe it's your mom or your dad. Maybe it's one of your siblings or a special friend. Perhaps it's one of your pets. Visualize a picture of that person. As I say the words out loud, visualize that you are saying these four phrases to that person:

May you be happy.
May you be healthy.
May you feel loved.
May you be safe.

(Repeat 1x)

It's so important to practice Metta on ourselves, as well as practice it on those that we love.

Now here comes the hardest, but most important, part of Metta: To spread love and kindness to those that we don't like very much.

It's important to practice Metta on people that we don't like very much because often they don't feel loved, happy, healthy, or safe.

So bring to mind someone you don't like very much. Maybe it's someone who has been unkind to you. Maybe it is someone who has hurt you, or maybe it is someone you love very much but have difficulty getting along with. Visualize yourself saying these four phrases to that person as I say them out loud:

May you be happy.
May you be healthy.
May you feel loved.
May you be safe.

(Repeat 1x)

When we practice Metta on someone who has been unkind to us, we often feel better, and we act with more love, compassion, and kindness to those around us. Remember that you can practice Metta anytime that you want to. All you need to do is use the four phrases, and see a picture in your mind of that person.

Now slowly begin to wiggle your fingers and toes, bringing awareness back to your physical body . . .

Listening to Yourself

+ A gentle practice in learning to listen to yourself and others without judgement or action.

Lie down on your back. Take a moment to make yourself comfortable and relaxed. Close your eyes and bring your attention to your breath. Breathe in as deeply as you can, then pause for a moment before letting your breath out in a calm, slow exhale. Continue breathing deeply in through your nose, feeling the cool air flow all the way down to your belly, and then slowly exhale it out.

As you lie in stillness and listen to my words, think about how good it feels to let yourself be calm and quiet in the middle of a long, busy day.

We don't often allow ourselves to rest and just be. We are often hurrying from one activity to the next — from home, to school, to a sports practice, or to a friend's house — busy living our full and happy lives.

It feels good to play and be productive and have friends; but it's also important that we practice learning how to slow down and listen to our bodies after a busy day.

That is what we are going to practice right now; learning to listen to what is happening inside of ourselves when we are calm and still.

Continue to take deep breaths in and out through your nose. Notice how your breath feels as it moves from your nose, down the back of your throat, and deep into your belly. Make sure your belly is moving up and down slowly as you breathe in . . . and out.

Listen for a moment to all the sounds you hear happening around you. Maybe you hear sounds in this room — such as the quiet breathing of others near you, the rustle of bodies shifting, or soft music playing.

Maybe you can hear the faint sounds of things outside of the room — such as people talking, cars driving, or birds singing. Whatever you hear is perfectly fine — you are safe and at peace inside this room. With your eyes still closed, identify all the sounds you hear right now.

Perhaps all you hear is silence. Silence has a special sound all its own.

Continue taking deep, peaceful breaths and turn your attention to the sounds you hear within yourself. Listen very carefully.

Can you hear your heart beating?

Can you hear the breath entering and leaving your body?

What else can you hear? Is your tummy making noises? Listen closely enough and you will hear the healthy energy pulsing through your veins — the energy that keeps you your strongest, best self.

Turn your attention now back to your breath. Listen carefully to your inhales and exhales.

The sound of your breath is magical. Your breath is the energy that flows in and out of your body keeping you alive.

Whenever you are feeling nervous, confused, or sad, you can focus on the sound of your breath and you will know that you are safe and you are okay, because you are alive.

Try to spend a little time each day focusing on your breath and listening to the sounds inside of yourself. Listen to your heart, your thoughts, and your feelings. Just listen to these things without needing to do anything in response. Listening to yourself is a very powerful thing to do.

Take another deep inhale . . . and exhale. Keep listening inside yourself as you breathe in . . . and out.

On your next exhale, begin to wiggle your fingers and your toes. Make small circles with your ankles and wrists, being sure to rotate them in both directions. Softly rock your head side to side, and then bend your knees and hug them into your chest.

Rock your whole body side to side, and then gently fall over to your right. Stay here for a moment, tucked into a small ball, and thank yourself for this practice today.

Take another deep inhale, and on your exhale, bring yourself up to a seated position.

Letting Go Meditation

+ A restorative visualization allowing yourself the time and space to just be.

Find a space on the floor to settle your body. Lie on your back. Stretch your legs long and rest your arms at your sides.

Begin to take deep inhales and exhales. Close your eyes or soften your gaze. Feel your mind, body, and breath begin to let go of any worries or unnecessary thoughts you've been holding on to. Inhale . . . and exhale.

Feel your heartbeat begin to slow . . . your shoulders relax . . . your face soften. Inhale . . . and exhale. Let your breathing become deeper.

Breathe into your belly, causing it to rise. Breathe out and feel the muscles in your body let go of any tension that is still there. Feel them becoming soft and relaxed.

There's nothing that you need to do here. You are free. There is nowhere else you need to be except right here, right now.

Relax your belly; let it grow big each time you breathe in, and then fall as you exhale.

Relax your forehead; let your brow be smooth and soft. Relax your chest . . . relax your belly.

Imagine you are floating in space and your body's tension is being melted away by the sun's soft rays. Imagine the sun is giving you power — it is filling you up with power. It is a power that is soaking through your skin. A power that you are absorbing with every cell of your body; from your toes to your hands to the top of your head.

Relax your whole body. Relax your feet . . . your legs. Relax your hands . . . your arms. Relax your back . . . your shoulders . . . your neck. Relax your face . . . your forehead. Relax the crown of your head.

Become aware now of all the empty space around you. It's very calm and very peaceful. It feels good.

I want you to imagine now that you are filling the space around you; that you have expanded beyond your body. Your energy is expanding broader and broader to fill up the room.

Right now you can forget about everything. You can forget the To-Do list, forget the stress. You can forget all your family's needs for this moment and just expand your body and your energy until that is all there is.

Fill the space around you until you feel so light and peaceful that you are floating. Floating through space, passing stars, huge planets and moons. Drifting . . . a million twinkling bright stars are all around you.

You are so happy and free right now floating through space. All that exists is you and your smile . . . and two big wide eyes looking out, observing the amazing vast universe. Just keep drifting, experiencing . . . and letting go.

Inhale . . . and exhale. Drifting . . . floating. When you're ready, slowly start to come back.

Begin to imagine your body floating down towards Earth. Further and further down you float as your energy flows back into your body and your body regains its normal size. Feel your body once again touching the earth.

Take another deep breath in . . . and out; then gently open your eyes, smile, and stretch.

Love Your Body Meditation

This mindfulness practice reminds you to appreciate your body for all the amazing things it allows you to do.

Close your eyes and take in a deep breath. Feel your belly rise as the air fills your lungs. Gently let it out. Take another deep breath in; hold it for a moment . . . then let it out.

Continue to breathe deeply in and out. As you breathe, allow your thoughts to grow quiet in your mind. There is nowhere else you need to be other than right here. Give yourself permission to be here; breathing deeply to calm your body and mind.

Feel your entire body getting warm and comfortable as you inhale...and exhale. Rest in this peaceful state and focus your mind on my words and the images that appear in your imagination. Today, we are going to learn something important about our amazing bodies.

In your mind, visualize a picture of yourself standing tall and strong. Perhaps you are outside in a grassy field, or you are standing inside your favorite room in your house. Wherever you imagine yourself to be, picture your strongest, healthiest self.

Your body is an amazing thing. It is made up of trillions of cells that work together to keep you healthy and strong. Can you imagine all those little cells working together in harmony to keep you at your very best?

Picture your bare feet. Think about each individual toe and the tops of your feet. Wiggle your toes in your mind and smile. Your feet and toes help you move from place to place. They let you run, skip, hop, and dance. Your feet have incredible capabilities. In your mind, thank them for empowering you to move and get where you want to go.

Now visualize your strong legs. Picture your shins, your knees, and the tops of your legs. Everybody's legs look different. Think about the color of your skin, and any marks you might have on your legs. Do you have freckles or a birthmark? Do you have bruises from playing hard?

Think about the muscles in your legs. They let you swim, kick, and jump. Everyone's legs look different, and everyone's legs are beautiful. Thank your legs for supporting you as you move through life.

Now picture your hands. Think about your fingers and the backs of your hands . . . think about your palms. Visualize wiggling your fingers and opening and closing your hands. Just like the rest of you, your hands are unique. Maybe your fingers are long, or maybe they are short. Maybe your hands are freckled, or maybe they have a small scar. What do your hands look like?

Your hands are wonderfully yours, and they allow you to do so many things. They let you hold a pencil to write, to hold hands with friends, and to catch a ball. They allow you to hold onto the things you love. Take a moment to be thankful for your hands and all they help you to do.

It is important to remember how special our physical bodies are. Your body allows you to live life in so many amazing ways, and nobody else in the world looks exactly like you. You are the only you, and that is a wonderful thing. You are beautiful and perfect just as you are.

Think about your arms now. Nobody else's arms look like yours, and your arms allow you to hug the people you love. Think about your shoulders and your back. The muscles in your upper body help you to climb on the playground and do cartwheels on the grass. They allow you to carry your favorite toys, books, and stuffed animals when you want to bring them from place to place. Thank your arms, your shoulders, and your back for helping you to be so strong.

Finally, think about your face. Think about your eyes, the color of your hair, and your smile. Picture your nose in the center of your face and the color of your skin. Your face allows people to recognize you in a crowded room or at a busy park. No one else looks like you — you are truly one-of-a-kind, and you are beautiful because you are you.

Smile now and imagine sending love to each and every part of your body, from the top of your head to the the tips of your toes. Be grateful for all the amazing things your body allows you to do.

Begin to wiggle your fingers and toes now, bringing awareness back to your body. Make small circles with your ankles and your wrists . . . first one way, then pausing to circle them in the other direction. Softly rock your head from side to side, carefully bringing movement into your neck.

Bend your knees and pull them tightly into your chest. Give yourself a great big hug — an expression of self-love. Roll gently onto your right side, and then in a way that is kind to your growing body, bring yourself up to a seated position with your hands at heart center.

Mindset Meditation

Lie on your back and relax your body. Straighten your legs and allow your feet to fall open naturally. Rest your arms at your sides or on your belly. Feel your shoulders and spine melt into the earth. Softly close your eyes.

Remember to come to your breath and take deep inhales and exhales in and out through your nose. Feel your whole body — from the top of your head to the tips of your toes — relax as your heartbeat slows with your breath. Listen to my words and focus on taking deep breaths in and out through your nose.

Inside your head is your big, beautiful brain. Your brain is incredibly important — it is the boss of your whole body. Your brain is very intelligent and it does so many things. It tells your heart to beat and your lungs to breathe. It tells your feet to run and tells your hands how to write the words on a page.

Your brain is where you think your thoughts and where you store your memories. Your brain is also in charge of your emotions. Your brain does so many amazing things.

Visualize your very busy brain working inside your head right now. It is lighting up with all of your thoughts while telling your body what to do to keep you healthy and safe. One of the tasks it's telling your body to do right now is to continue to take deep breaths in . . . and out. To inhale . . . and exhale.

Did you know that your brain is like a muscle? The harder it has to work at something, the stronger it gets. Problems and challenges in school are like weights at the gym for your brain. If you want your brain to get bigger and stronger, you have to lift the heavier weights.

This means that in school, when you choose to work on a challenge instead of a simpler problem, your brain grows and gets stronger. It might feel uncomfortable at times to work on something that makes you struggle rather than choosing the easier task, but it is the healthiest thing you can do for your brain.

Your brain also enjoys making mistakes. Mistakes are how it learns new things — and your brain loves to learn. Take another deep inhale . . . and exhale while you think about this.

When you do something that your brain already knows how to do — like writing your name or brushing your teeth — you don't usually make mistakes. This is because these are easy tasks that you have already learned. But your brain is not learning or growing when it does familiar things because it already knows how to do those tasks.

When you learn something new, you might start off by making mistakes. This is great because when you make a mistake, your brain is simply learning how to do the new skill the right way the next time. Mistakes are really learning opportunities for your brain to grow and get stronger.

So the next time you make a mistake while you are learning something new — celebrate! You have created a learning opportunity and are one step closer to learning how to do things better the next time.

Take another deep inhale . . . and exhale. An inhale . . . and an exhale. Know that your brain is doing what it needs right now to keep you healthy and safe. Take a moment to visualize your brain flexing its muscles when it is challenged, and think about something you can do today to help your brain to grow.

Breathe in . . . and out.

In . . . and out.

Feel how calm and relaxed your body is as you breathe . . . how healthy it feels to rest like this. Gently begin to wiggle your fingers and your toes, awakening yourself back to the present.

Continue to breathe as you make soft circles with your ankles and your wrists; first one way, then pausing to reverse them in the other direction. Take a deep inhale and hug your knees into your chest.

Squeeze yourself into the tightest ball that you can; then release to stretch yourself long before bringing yourself up to a seated position for our close of practice.

Tense & Release Muscle Relaxation

+ A restorative visualization allowing yourself the time and space to just be.

Make your body comfortable. Lie on your back with your legs stretched long and your hands resting at your sides. Take a deep breath in . . . and out. Close your eyes and allow your body to relax.

Today we are going to do a practice called a Tense and Release Muscle Relaxation to help our bodies feel as calm and relaxed as possible. I am going to guide you in how to use your breath, your muscles, and your positive thoughts to help relax your body from the tips of your toes all the way to the top of your head.

We'll begin with your feet. Curl your toes and squeeze the muscles in your feet as tightly as you can. Take a deep inhale while keeping your toes curled . . . then exhale and uncurl your toes to release. Let all the tension in your feet go as you take another deep inhale . . . and an exhale.

Now picture the lower parts of your legs — your calves and your shins — clearly in your mind. Imagine forcing your lower legs together as you tense the muscles there. Take a deep breath in as you continue to squeeze . . . and then exhale as you let all the tension go.

Do this for the muscles in your upper legs as well. Imagine forcing your legs together as you tense your legs above the knee. Squeeze tightly as you take a deep breath in . . . and then exhale as you let it go. Breathe and relax your body completely. Allow yourself to melt into the ground beneath you.

Now we are going to move on to your bottoms, or your "sit bones." Take a deep breath and squeeze all the muscles in your bottom together as tightly as you can. It might cause your body to lift off the ground a little. Squeeze tightly as you continue to breathe . . . and on your next exhale release. Feel all the muscles in your bottom relax as your body melts back into the ground beneath you.

Let's just focus on our breath for a moment here. Breathe in . . . and out. Inhale . . . and exhale.

Notice how your lower body feels. Does it feel more relaxed after having done this exercise? I hope so. If your eyes have opened during this activity, softly close them again. Let's move on to the rest of your body now, starting with your hands.

Continue to breathe, and squeeze your hands tightly into fists. Squeeze all the muscles in your hands as tightly as you can. Inhale and squeeze . . . then exhale and release. Uncurl your fingers and return your hands to rest, palms up, on the floor.

Now stiffen the muscles in your arms as though you were trying to force them together. Squeeze the muscles in your arms, maybe even making your arms shake with the effort, and then release and relax your arms back to the ground. Let your arms go limp, like noodles, as you let all the tension go. Continue to take deep breaths in and out through your nose as you allow your body to relax.

We are going to move on to your shoulders and back now. Take a deep inhale and squeeze the backs of your shoulders together while keeping your shoulders away from your ears. See if you can tense the muscles along your spine and into your lower back. Continue to squeeze and tense your shoulders and back as you breathe. Take a deep inhale . . . and as you exhale, let it all go.

Let your shoulders relax and feel your back melt into the floor. Enjoy how good it feels to just rest after holding on to that tension in your shoulders and your spine. Take deep breaths in and out as you continue to rest.

Finally, see if you can tense the back of your neck all the way up to the crown of your head. In your mind, visualize a golden rod of light stretching your head and neck long. Hold this stretch as you inhale, and as you exhale let it all go.

Your body is fully relaxed now. Your muscles are loose, and any tension you had been holding on to has melted away. Take a deep inhale . . . and exhale. Breathe in . . . and out.

You are at peace . . . calm and still. Feel your heartbeat slow even more with your deep breaths. Breathe in . . . and out. In . . . and out.

You can do this muscle relaxation exercise anytime you want to let go of any stress or worries you are holding in your body. You can do it lying in your bed, riding in the car, or sitting at your desk in school. Simply squeeze your muscles one at a time while you breathe . . . and then relax.

Begin to wiggle your fingers and toes, bringing movement back into your physical body. Rock your neck softly side to side, then reach your arms up over your head to make your body as long as you possibly can. Bend your knees and hug them tightly into your chest. Rock side to side, and then gently fall over onto your right. Bring yourself up to a seated position with your hands at heart center for our close of practice.

Melody of Meditation

Close your eyes. Take a deep breath in through your nose and out. Breathe in deeply, pause for a gentle heartbeat, then softly let it out.

Continue to take deep, slow breaths. Remember that when we slow our breath, we slow our hearts, and then we can slow our minds.

Continue to breathe in through your nose . . . and out.

Begin thinking about some of the thoughts that take up space in your mind. Identify some of the thoughts that you are having right now: Maybe they are thoughts of your mom or your dad, a sport that you play, an activity that is happening later today, or thoughts about what you're going to eat next. Your thoughts can be whatever they are.

Perhaps you have two very big thoughts that are taking up space in your mind. Maybe you have five small thought bubbles that are surrounding your head.

Somedays we have lots of thoughts racing through our brains, and sometimes we just have one or two big thoughts that take up all the space inside of our heads and our hearts.

Sometimes our thoughts can make us act differently than we want to. Sometimes our thoughts make us too excited, too sad, or very unfocused.

We often forget how powerful we are, and that we can make these thoughts that bother us POOF away. Let's practice how powerful we are. Let's make these thoughts disappear. Are you ready?

Look at five thoughts you are having right now. Maybe you see a word or a picture in your thought bubble. Visualize your thoughts however you want.

Let's look at the first thought. Make it disappear.

Now let's look at the second thought. Make it disappear.

What about the third thought? Can you make it disappear?

And the fourth thought? Make it disappear.

Is there a fifth thought? Make it disappear.

See how powerful you are? Now enjoy how your mind feels with all the thoughts cleared from your mind. Take five deep inhales with me, enjoying this clear space in your head.

Inhale . . . and exhale.

Inhale . . . and exhale.

Inhale . . . and exhale.

Inhale . . . and exhale.

Inhale . . . and exhale.

When you are ready, start to wiggle your fingers and toes to bring awareness back into your physical body. Take a nice big stretch with your arms reaching away from your feet. Make your body as long as you possibly can, and then in a way that is kind to your growing body, bring yourself up to a seated position for our close of practice.

Fill Your Bucket Mindfulness Practice

Inspired by the popular children's book, "*Have You Filled a Bucket Today?*", this meditation visualizes a bucket inside of each one of us. Our buckets are filled by kind words and actions, and are emptied when we feel hurt.

Close your eyes and take in a very deep breath. Breathe deeply in through your nose, and let it back out. Feel the air come in through your nose and flow all the way down into your belly. Feel your belly extend and rise as you breathe in, then feel your belly relax as you breathe out.

Turn your focus within, and listen very quietly to what you hear happening in your body. Can you hear your heart beating? Can you hear your own breath as you breathe slowly in . . . and out? Maybe your tummy is making noises, or perhaps it's very quiet within. Whatever is going on inside of you, just take the time to listen.

Imagine that inside of you there is a big, beautiful bucket. Everyone has one, although we can't see them with our eyes. When we feel good, our buckets are full. But when we are feeling bad, our buckets are low or even empty.

Did you know that when you fill someone else's bucket with kindness, helpfulness, or even a smile, your bucket gets filled up too? That's actually one of the ways we fill our own buckets: When we share goodness with others and think happy thoughts. Our buckets get filled to the top when we do this.

The other way our buckets get full is when others are kind to us with their actions and their words. When we receive kindness, our buckets get even fuller.

However, when unkind words are spoken, our buckets become a little emptier. This is true when we speak unkindly to others, and when others say unkind words to us. We all want our buckets to be full of love, kindness, peacefulness, and happiness . . . everyone does. So it is important that we always speak and act with kindness.

We can make a choice each and every day to show loving kindness to others to help fill up their buckets. When we do this, our buckets get filled too! They get filled to the top, and they can even overflow with happiness.

Now let's imagine for a moment a time when you might get upset with someone. What do you imagine is happening to your bucket when you are upset? What's happening to the other person's bucket? We don't want empty buckets because it doesn't feel nice inside. So your goal when you get upset is to talk about what you're feeling without using words that could empty your bucket, or anyone else's. You can do it. Just imagine that bucket, and keep filling it.

If your bucket ever feels low or empty, you can take in a deep breath and remember how loved you are. You can choose to be grateful for all the good things and people you have in your life, and focus on that. Remember, always, to let your bucket be full, and to fill other people's buckets as well.

When you're ready, take in one more deep inhale and exhale, and then give a big smile.

Fall Forest Meditation

✦ This seasonal visualization is a reminder that it is always best to let go of the things that don't help us to be our best selves.

Settle down onto your back. Make yourself comfortable with your hands at your sides or resting on your belly. Make your legs long and allow your feet to fall naturally apart. Close your eyes and take a deep breath in. Hold your inhale for a heartbeat, then softly let it out.

Continue to take deep inhales with slow, soft exhales. Focus on breathing in through your nose, and back out through your nose. If this isn't comfortable for you, however, breathe in the way that feels best for you right now. Feel your heart and mind begin to settle, and let your body completely relax as you breathe in . . . and out.

Let's do this three more times . . .

Breathe in . . . and out.
Breathe in . . . and out.
Breathe in . . . and out.

Imagine yourself walking down a well worn path in a tree-filled forest. It is an autumn day, and the air feels crisp and cool on your face. The path you are traveling on is a narrow winding dirt road with dry leaves and twigs that crunch beneath your feet. Sunlight filters through the rustling leaves overhead, illuminating your path in a dim glow.

The leaves on the trees have begun to change their colors for fall. They are a foliage of brilliant red, sunburnt orange, golden yellow, and deep burgundy. As you examine this colorful leafy canopy, you watch as a breeze lifts several leaves off of the branches and they slowly drift down onto the ground.

Autumn is a time to remember that sometimes in life it is best to let things go. In order to be our best selves, we need to let go of any worries, fears, or frustrations we have been holding on to.

Think quietly right now to yourself about anything in your life you have been holding on to that is not helping you to be your best self. Perhaps you have been angry at a friend for something they did that left you feeling sad or hurt. Maybe you have been fearful of trying something new at school because it seems too hard. Or perhaps you have a habit, like forgetting to clean your room or biting your nails, that you need to get rid of or change.

Whatever anger, fear, or frustration it is you have been holding on to, it is time to let it go. Picture whatever is holding you back as a leaf on one of the trees. As the next autumn breeze whispers through the forest, watch as that leaf flutters off the branch and falls softly to the ground.

Doesn't it feel good to let these things go?

If you can, think of something else that you want to let go of, and picture it as another leaf on the tree. As you exhale your next breath, see the air leave your body and whoosh into the forest to blow that leaf gently away.

Continue to take deep, calming inhales and exhales as you travel further down the winding dirt path inside the fall forest of your mind. You are in control here. You can let as many things go from your heart and your mind as you wish. Anything that has been making you sad, tired, or angry can become a colorful leaf that is blown away by the autumn wind.

Breathe in . . . and out.

Breathe in . . . and out.

Breathe in . . . and out.

Know that you can come back to this forest in your mind anytime you need to calm your mind or your body. You can also come back anytime you need a safe space to let go of the things in your life that aren't helping you to be your best self.

Take another inhale, and on your exhale begin to wiggle your fingers and toes to bring awareness back to your physical body. Gently open and close your hands and softly rock your head from side to side to carefully awaken your neck. Reach your arms overhead as far away from your feet as you possibly can to stretch your body long . . . and then bend your knees and hug them into your chest.

Rock your whole body from side to side, and then let yourself gently fall over to the left. Stay here, tucked like a caterpillar inside a cocoon, for just a moment before bringing yourself up to a seated position. Bring your hands to your heart center and take another deep inhale as we prepare for our close of practice.

Winter Rest Meditation

Take a deep breath in through your nose, and out. Close your eyes and begin to connect your slowing heart to a calm, restful body.

I'm going to count down from five to one, and when I get to one, your whole body will feel very heavy and deeply relaxed. You will feel so calm and peaceful you won't even want to move. When you get to this point, allow yourself to stay still and enjoy the rest your body needs and deserves.

5 . . . bring your attention to your arms and your legs. Release any tension you have been holding here.

4 . . . your legs are starting to feel heavy, and your arms too. Let them sink into the ground.

3 . . . continue to breathe, and allow your shoulders to melt into the earth. Release any lingering tension you have been holding; moving from the top of your spine, to your lower back, all the way to the bottoms of your feet.

2 . . . your body grows heavier and heavier; more and more relaxed with each number that I say.

1 . . . your whole body is now still and at peace.

In your mind, imagine an empty field covered in snow. It is a cold winter's day. The sky is gray, the trees are bare, nothing is stirring. A quiet stillness hangs in the air.

Winter is a time of rest. It is when plants sleep under the ground, animals tuck safely inside their nests, and the whole world moves at a much slower pace.

The earth needs this time of rest — a chance to recover before the business of spring reawakens the world. It is during this time of winter that the soil, the plants, and the animals rest and restore their energy for the busy Spring days that lie ahead.

Just like the earth, people need periods of rest in order to nurture and restore themselves. We can't be at our very best if we are tired and run down. In order to be our best selves, we need to learn to lie still and be calm. It is during these periods of deep rest that our muscles and our brains grow; and when it is quiet, we are able to hear the truths that lie deep inside of our hearts.

So rest now. Allow your body to be heavy and melt into the earth as you continue to take deep breaths in . . . and out. Breathe in . . . and out.

(Allow several minutes of silence, or as long as appropriate)

It is now time to reawaken your physical body. Gently wiggle your fingers and toes. Make small circles with your ankles and wrists; first one way . . . and then in the opposite direction. Softly shake your head as though saying, "No," and then nod it as though saying, "Yes." Reach your arms up overhead as though you are reaching for the sky, and then bend your knees and hug them into your chest. Squeeze yourself tightly, and then roll onto one side before bringing yourself up to a seated position with your hands at heart center.

Springtime Garden

✚ This visualization set in a spring garden reflects on the importance of new beginnings and fresh starts.

Lie down on the floor with your legs loose and long. Relax your arms by your sides or bring your hands to gently rest on your belly. Close your eyes and take a deep breath in to clear your mind and open your heart.

Imagine walking down a lovely, winding outdoor path. It is late spring; the grass is green and the sun shines in a clear blue sky. Birds chirp merrily from nearby trees. The air smells of fresh earth and newly cut grass. Breathe deeply to inhale the air around you, and feel the warm sun on your skin.

Continue walking down the path until you come upon a low stone wall. There is a gate in the wall, and inside is the most beautiful garden you have ever seen.

You open the gate and step inside. What do you see? This is your garden — it can be however you want it to be. What colors of flowers do you see? Pink, blue, yellow, purple?

Are there trees inside to create shade for your garden, or is your garden cloaked in sunlight? Are there vegetables growing in your garden? Is there a fountain sprinkling water, or perhaps a stream running down the middle?

Take the time to imagine your garden with as much detail as possible. Are there friendly animals inside, or a pleasant place to sit? Picture the garden of your dreams clearly in your mind.

Spring is a time of renewal, of fresh starts. It is when the flowers and plants that were sleeping all winter emerge from the earth to bloom. It is when new grass grows and baby animals are born. Spring represents hope and new beginnings.

Just like nature in the springtime, our lives are filled with fresh starts and opportunities to begin again. Every day we are given multiple chances to be the absolute best versions of ourselves we can be.

Each morning when we wake up, we get to decide what kind of attitude we want to have and what types of choices we want to make that day.

When we find ourselves in the middle of the afternoon, acting in ways that don't reflect the best version of ourselves, we have the power to hit pause, take a deep breath, and redirect our own behaviors.

At night, when reflecting on the long, busy day you had, you can think about all the good choices you made that day, while also deciding how you can be an even better version of yourself tomorrow.

Isn't it refreshing to know that we get to determine our own behaviors and give ourselves a fresh start any time we need? We always have the power to hit reset on our lives so that we can act with more kindness, thoughtfulness, and integrity with the next word we speak or action we take.

Think about your garden once again, and select your favorite spot in the garden to sit. Visualize yourself calm and at peace as you enjoy all the beauty your garden has to offer. Breathe deeply to inhale the fresh, spring air, and then softly let it out.

Breathe in . . . and out.

Breathe in . . . and out.

One more breath in . . . and out.

Gently start to wiggle your fingers and toes, preparing to bring your physical body back to the present. Continue to breathe, then point your toes and stretch your arms up and out behind you, reaching the tips of your fingers as far away from the tips of your toes as you can. Take a deep inhale to make your body as long as possible, and then exhale and bring your arms back to your sides.

Softly shake your head side to side, as though saying no, then bend your knees and hug them into your chest. Rock your whole body side to side, allowing yourself to fall over to one side or the other. Take a few more breaths in this cocoon-like position, and when you are ready, bring yourself up to a seated position for our close of practice.

Summer Cloud Meditation

This guided mindfulness practice, set in a sunny field on a summer day, is a reflection on how our thoughts and feelings are constantly changing.

Lie down on your back. Take a moment to make yourself comfortable and relaxed. Close your eyes and bring your attention to your breath. Breathe in as deeply as you can, then pause for a moment before letting your breath out in a calm, slow exhale.

Imagine in your mind a warm summer day. You are in the middle of a large green field, lying on your back atop a soft blanket in the grass. The sky stretches out in front of you . . . an endless expanse of brilliant blue.

The warm sun soaks into every inch of your skin, filling you from head to toe with its heat. You feel completely comfortable, relaxed, and content.

As you watch the blue sky overhead, a large puffy white cloud drifts across. Imagine this cloud clearly in your mind. What does it look like? What shape does it form? You watch as the cloud slowly drifts across the sky until you can't see it any longer. The sky is once again empty and blue.

As you continue to gaze up at the sky, another cloud emerges, this one completely different from the last. What does this cloud look like? How big is it? Is it soft and fluffy, or thin and wispy? Picture the cloud clearly in your mind.

As you watch this cloud drift across the sky, it slowly changes its shape. It grows and expands, then shifts and shrinks. By the time this cloud has traveled from one side of the sky to the next, it looks completely different. Soon it, too, travels so far away that you can't see it anymore.

You continue to lie on your back, taking deep breaths in and out through your nose as you watch the clouds travel across the blue sky. Each cloud is different, and slowly changes its shape as it floats by overhead. Each cloud eventually disappears when it drifts too far away in the sky.

This is so relaxing.

Your thoughts are like the clouds that drift across a summer sky. Each thought you have is different from the next. Some thoughts enter and leave quickly, while others stay and linger longer in your mind. Thoughts also change as they travel through our brains, just like clouds change as they drift across the sky.

Some thoughts even come into our minds like storm clouds — dark, thunderous, and gray. These storm clouds thoughts are louder than the other thoughts we have, and they often don't feel very good. Just like all thoughts that enter our minds, though, these storm cloud thoughts will eventually leave — or even change into calm, peaceful clouds — if we give them enough time. We just have to be patient.

Clouds are wonderful, strange, and beautiful, but they are not permanent. Neither are our thoughts. Thoughts come and go and change over time. Our job is to watch our thoughts, like clouds in the sky, without judgment or strong reactions.

Take another deep breath in through your nose . . . then softly let it out. Feel the warm summer sun soaking through your skin one final time before beginning to wiggle your fingers and toes. Start to awaken yourself to the present and make small circles with your ankles and wrists . . . first one direction, and then the other.

Make small movements with your neck, then reach your arms up overhead to stretch your entire body as long as you can. Bend your knees and hug them into your chest. Roll over onto one side, and then bring yourself up to a seated position for our close of practice.

Tree Meditation

Close your eyes and take a deep breath in. Feel the air move all the way into your belly before softly letting it out. Take another deep breath in, once again feeling the air move all the way inside your belly, and then softly let it out.

Allow your entire body to grow heavy and sink into the earth. Loosen the muscles in your legs . . . in your waist and your tummy . . . in your shoulders and arms . . . in your neck . . . and let the top of your head fall back into the ground. Be completely relaxed as you imagine yourself outside on a clear, sunny day.

Take in another deep breath to smell the fresh air around you, and then exhale it out. Continue to take deep breaths as you imagine the sun in the sky and the grass at your feet. Hear the whisper of a gentle wind blowing and birds softly singing in the distance.

It is safe here, and very peaceful.

Bring your attention back to your body and visualize yourself as a tall, healthy tree in nature. Imagine your feet rooting down into the earth. Picture your feet growing and extending, like actual tree roots, down, down, to anchor you into the ground. Your roots connect you deeply and strongly to the earth. They are your values, beliefs, and the loved ones in your life that keep you anchored to who you are as a person.

Now visualize your legs and torso as the trunk of your tree rising out of the earth. The trunk of your tree is firm as it rises up and up towards the sky. Your trunk is strong and solid. How does the bark on your tree trunk feel? Is it soft and smooth, or is it bumpy and rough? Imagine how the trunk of your tree would feel if you ran your hand across its surface.

Take another deep inhale, and then an exhale. Inhale . . . and exhale.

Imagine your arms now as the branches of your tree reaching and expanding towards the sky. Spread your fingers and stretch your palms and picture them covered with leaves rustling in the breeze. These leafy limbs breathe in your oxygen and absorb the sun's warm energy. Your branches offer shade on sunny days and shelter from drizzling rain clouds.

Take a deep breath in and feel your body extend long. Feel the crown of your head as the very top of your tree that can see all around you. What does it see? Are there fields of grass? A forest of trees? Are you near a stream of running water? Take in all the details of the land stretching out around you.

As you continue to take deep, mindful breaths, notice what is happening inside your tree. Begin at the tips of your roots and work up to your trunk and then into your branches, twigs, and leaves. Feel your presence, strength, and flexibility. Your tree is very wise . . . it knows you are safely and securely rooted to the earth, yet you also know how to bend and sway in stormy weather in order to survive.

Think about all the life that you connect with as a tree. Think about how these creatures depend on you for survival. You are important.

Think about all the wisdom you absorb in your life as a tree. What message does your tree have for you?

When you are ready, slowly start to bring your awareness back from every part of your tree to the present. Draw yourself out of the roots. Come back up from the ground, and back from the branches, leaves, and trunk.

Wiggle your fingers and toes. Move your ankles and wrists. Bend your knees and hug them into your chest. Gently roll onto the right side of your body. Take a deep inhale to return fully into your body.

With your eyes still closed, listen to the sounds around you. Remember the message your tree told you. Then open your eyes and bring yourself up to a seated position for our close of practice.

CHALLENGE TO CHANGE INC.

Challenge to Change Inc. offers signature Mindfulness programming for all ages. As a former educator, Molly Schreiber, founder and owner of Challenge to Change, keeps teachers and learners at the heart of her mission. Therefore, much of Challenge to Change's programming and resources were designed to support the happiness and health of children, teens, parents, and teachers. Located in Dubuque, Iowa, Challenge to Change spreads its mission far and wide through the use of virtual yoga classes, online training sessions, literature, and online resources.

A Classroom in Balance's 100 Mindfulness practices are featured virtually through our online platform **Yoga and Mindfulness Portal**. Visit challengetochangeinc.com for more information.

RESOURCES

Our easy-to-use Yoga and Mindfulness resources were developed for use in a classroom, studio, or home setting.

TRAININGS

Our 95 Hour, 200 Hour, and 300 Hour Yoga Teacher Training programs empower teachers, parents, and yogis alike to share the practices of Yoga and Mindfulness with toddlers, kids, teens, and adults.

CONTINUING EDUCATION

These courses were designed to help classroom teachers find ways to meaningfully integrate Mindfulness within their school day in a way that best serves their students and meets their scheduling needs.

PROGRAMMING

Challenge to Change's most popular program is The Yoga in the Schools Project, which provides meaningful thirty minute lessons that support the social-emotional growth of students. Our mission offers in-person lessons locally around Dubuque, IA, as well as virtual programming for our more distant learning communities.

CLASSES AND WORKSHOPS

We are always exploring new ways to share Yoga, Mindfulness, and Meditation practices with others. Join us for an in-person or virtual class or workshop. We offer sound healing, family yoga, personalized yoga classes, children's camps, yoga birthday parties, and more.

Learn more about our mission, meet the team, and explore our resources at

www.challengetochangeinc.com

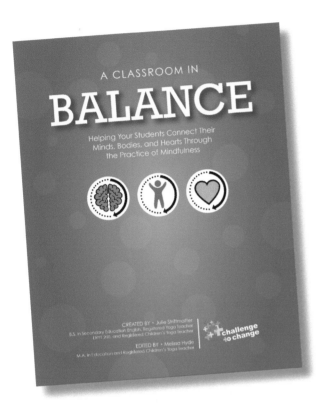

Smart Mind,
Kind Heart,
Calm Body
BY • Molly Schreiber

Smart Mind, Kind Heart, Calm Body teaches readers several new mindfulness practices to use when faced with strong emotions and uncomfortable situations. It shows how we can be in charge of our thoughts and our reactions when we use the practice of mindfulness.

Change The Station
In Your Brain
BY • Molly Schreiber

Change the Station in Your Brain teaches young children that they have the power to create a positive mindset by connecting to their breath with positive affirmations and mantras.

CPSIA information can be obtained
at www.ICGtesting.com
Printed in the USA
LVHW071901171121
703473LV00002B/106